EXACTLY WHAT
HAPPENED

EXACTLY
WHAT
HAPPENED

Joel Brouwer

12·16·99

To Richard,

With thanks and admiration.

Joel

PURDUE UNIVERSITY PRESS / WEST LAFAYETTE, INDIANA

03 02 01 00 99   5 4 3 2 1

The paper used in this book meets the minimum requirements
of American National Standard for Information Sciences—
Permanence of Paper for Printed Library Materials, ANSI Z39.48-1992.

∞™

Printed in the United States of America
Design by inari

Library of Congress Cataloging-in-Publication Data

Brouwer, Joel, 1968–
Exactly what happened / Joel Brouwer.
p. cm.
ISBN 1-55753-158-7 (paper : alk. paper)
I. Title.
PS3552.R68245E83   1999
811'.54—dc21   99-27481
CIP

to Francine

Ceaselessly musing, venturing, throwing, seeking . . .

Who are you going to believe, me or your own eyes?

—Chico Marx, in *Duck Soup*

CONTENTS

III

I

The map of Espejismo County in the September 3 edition should not have included the town of Black Arrow. There is no such place.

— The Grisbee (Arizona) Bee
September 10, 1988

ABRACADABRA KIT

Because the Evil Knights, who chewed Skoal
in sixth grade and wore matching black jackets,
beat me to jelly almost every day,
the joy buzzers, pepper gum, and fake puke
on offer in Batman's sooty back pages
seemed meager, trifling, idle junk. Even
the X-ray specs which turned skirts clear left me
cold: so you see their panties. Then what?
All these were mere pranks. I needed power.

And so with the last of my birthday cash
I ordered the Abracadabra Kit.
The ad promised rivals would flee me in terror
and pictured grownups swooning (eyes X's)
as a boy in tails drove swords through his sister.
I checked the mailbox every day and dreamed
the damage I'd do the Knights, the magic words
I'd speak to blanket them with zits, shrivel
their cocks, cripple their families and pets.

The kit came and of course was crap.
Three thimbles and a marble for the shell game,
a wand which bloomed paper roses just once
before its spring broke, a hank of clothesline
for knot tricks. Most useless of all, a book:
43 *Illusions for Beginners.*
The book said *people need magic more than water.*
The book said *practice* and *takes years to master.*
Sent to bed at ten, I read, rapt, by flashlight.

The next day at recess the chief Knight, Pete,
brought me a dog turd, said *Here's your lunch, fag.*
I reached, pulled an egg from his ear, cracked it
in my hand, and mom's canary shot up
gold between us, pulsed above the playground,
vanished whistling over the gym. That instant—
Pete's gulp of wonder before his first savage punch
hooked my gut, the bird flying wild and oblivious—
my haven then, my labor ever since.

SNOW

*One winter, when much snow fell in Florence,
Piero de'Medici caused Michelangelo to make
him in his courtyard a statue of snow, which
was very beautiful.*

—Vasari's *Lives*

He found his rasps and hammers useless,
too crude for such soft stone.
So he chiseled the head

with his fingers: scratched ice
from the ears, rubbed his numb palms
against the cheeks to smooth them.

He stood on a ladder with his back
to the balcony, so the Medicis' guests
could not see the statue's face take shape.

Clots of snow flew from his fingers,
dropped to the ground. The guests
amused themselves by guessing what magic

might be forming behind his black cloak.
Bacchus? Moses? Maybe the Pope?
After an hour, bored, they ordered the artist

to step aside. We cannot know
what they saw. Vasari doesn't say. But let's imagine
that silence falls thick as a blizzard

on the crowd. That the children drop
toys and hide behind their mothers.
That every eye wanders

up the snowman's bright muscles,
his dazzling, impossible flesh,
and locks to his lucid gaze,

which seems so certain, so candid,
that the guests shiver, look away,
turn suddenly solemn.

Later, at the feast, a young woman slips
from the table and rushes
to the courtyard, where a stray warm wind

strokes the statue's face, erasing
each feature. She climbs the ladder, stands
nose to nose, staring hard as if

the force of her looking will bring the face,
already so close to life,
to life. She scrapes away the thick, curved lips,

squeezes them between her hands.
She dribbles the liquid into a small glass vial,
which she'll wear on a necklace,

the water exactly as warm as her skin.
She imagines that strong, ruthless mouth
still beautiful, pressing heavy against her.

"ASTRONOMERS DETECT WATER IN DISTANT GALAXY, SUGGEST LIFE MAY BE PRESENT THROUGHOUT UNIVERSE"

— *The San Francisco Chronicle* April 3, 1994

Whether a thimbleful frozen hard as a tooth
or a boiling lagoon they don't say.
Because it doesn't matter. A single drop

or an ocean makes the same implication,
namely: maybe. Maybe we're not alone
in this universe, friends. Maybe bathtubs

up there, bougainvillea and thunderheads.
And maybe (why not?) they've got it
good up there: no mumps, no smashed china

on the kitchen floor, no rubber checks
to the gas company, no Kalashnikovs . . .
Beleaguered skeptics everywhere, you may begin

dreaming now. Of wars fought with peonies,
or glasses of milk. Of every belly filled each day
with dish after succulent dish. Of law books

one sentence long: "Be nice." But maybe this
is too much to hope. Perhaps
they're just protozoa up there, wiggling

blind in a sullen puddle. Let's rocket there quick
and help them avoid our mistakes,
snatch the stone from their first murderer's hand,

inoculate them for plague and smallpox,
burn their Oppenheimer's notes. In a few million years
they could be perfect, with our help,

and then we could go live there too, simply,
in cabañas along the ocean, eating mangoes
and staring out at the deep blue water, wondering

when somewhere out there the first shark
will feel its first tooth
rise like a dagger from its jaw.

THE FOREIGN CORRESPONDENT

kneels in red dust to unpack his camera.
Swarms of children, bellies swollen with air,
poke his ridiculous pale skin. The dead

are piled at the edge of town, awaiting
the Red Cross backhoe. Someone's thrown a dog
on top of the heap. The correspondent focuses

on a woman's slack face. Her earrings glare,
and he stoops to remove them.
He once believed his job was only to see,

to be a third eye for those of us hungry for more
than a meager pair can provide. He would haunt
the world, its cardboard slums and firefights,

its brambled clearings where hooded men
dump bones on moonless nights, snapping fact
after fact for our review. But he soon learned

the ropes: skip the fill-flash
and the starving man's eyes sink back
into poignant shadow. The beggar with one coin

in his cup has more punch than the cripple with ten.
If the earrings glare, unhook them.
Years ago, to celebrate his first assignment,

he gave his wife a pair of diamond earrings
and she asked him to put them in. His hands shook
at the intimacy of it—the down on pink flesh,

the delicate wound. That same night she gave him
a stainless steel canteen: *For my photographic
Marco Polo.* On the way to the airport he stopped

to bang the flask against a flagpole, scour away
its greenhorn shine with pebbles and dirt. Now he pinches
this empty ear in his fingers, twists the bright clasp.

"FORMER KENYAN PARLIAMENT MEMBER ARRESTED FOR 'IMAGINING THE DEATH' OF PRESIDENT DANIEL ARAP MOI"

— The New York Times October 1, 1995

I imagine him behind a desk big as a Buick, irked
the administration's blocked his hydroelectric
or plastics factory scheme, and the idea, unsummoned, arrives
in his mind: the President's head gone in a cloud of blood.

And then the police are there. They smoke his cigarettes
while he finds his coat, and across town a jailer mops down
the concrete floor of a cell, his radio muttering weather . . .
It could have happened otherwise: this is just imagination.

The same one which last night handed me, unasked,
a vision of an ex as I watched my wife undress—
her true legs and shoulders haunted by misty others,
a ghost spine arched like a cobra in her back—

while I gawked like a traffic-accident rubbernecker,
half-fascinated, half-ashamed, though my actual hands
were clean as this daydreaming Kenyan's,
each of us innocent as a fresco of Judas on a chapel wall.

My ninth-grade Bible teacher claimed thinking the sin
was just as bad as sinning. This seemed to me untrue.
Who was wounded when I pictured the class bully stabbed,
or dreamed my drama teacher nude and willing?

What delicious lack of consequence! What fool would refuse
to swap for it his citizenship in the tangible?
Certainly not our Kenyan un-murderer, now lashed to a chair
in his cell. He imagines himself, let's say, in Florence,

about to emerge from the Uffizi into a plaza stunned
with autumn's blaring sun. See how he pauses at the threshold?
Each time he steps over, the truncheons of the actual
blast again like an avalanche across his broken legs.

LT. SHRAPNEL

Here's to Lieutenant (eventually General) Henry Shrapnel,
inventor in 1784 of a shell designed to burst
above the enemy's head and so return to earth
not in the traditional singular plop but a swarm
of hissing steel bits, each with force enough to pierce
flesh simply as a drillbit twisting through butter.

No more lobbing awkward hunks of lead and praying
one crashed dumbly down on the bad guy's head;
Shrapnel sweetened the odds of kill by a million.
While the brass hatched plans to smush the enemy
utterly *(Let's catapult boulders! Let's sprinkle
their position with bricks!)* or rip away whole chunks

of his flesh at once *(Here's a bullet big as a trashcan!),*
the Lt. pondered the tender swamp of our insides:
needle a glint of steel between a guy's ribs, he figured,
and it will snip him to chop suey from the inside out.
This switch in thinking—*elephant* to *gnat, gnat, gnat*—
began the era of military insidiousness: cannonballs

and boiling oil became passé, mustard gas and frag mines
all the rage, until at last we coaxed omega from alpha:
whole cities gone smoke and shadow from half an atom.
Shrapnel: inventor of our century some hundred years early.
Shrapnel: who taught us to kill capillary by capillary
and dig the deepest graves with a million tiny shovels.

LOCKING UP THE RUSSIAN

His wife had left for good the day before,
citing his drinking and lack of *Get-up-go*.
Now the unemployed Russian from downstairs,
drunk on my gin on my porch, said *I am not drunk*.

Listen to me. If she does not come back
my heart maybe breaks, maybe it does not.
If yes, it breaks, you are my friend
and yes, you will lock me in my room.

All summer I'd questioned the Russian
about suffering. I need to know, I told him,
how it feels to suffer. I need to know this
so I can write books. But the Russian

would only laugh, shake his head, and ask
if anyone was using that sandwich.
It was his favorite joke. *Is anyone using*
this cigarette? Are you using that beer?

That week he seemed fine. He went fishing all day
and gulped dozens of my unused olives at night.
But one drunk midnight on the porch, the street
so still I could hear the power lines hum,

the Russian spoke from the darkness: *Friend,*
yes, now you lock me in my room. I laughed,
but he raised himself from his chair with a groan
and slapped me on the knee, as if our break

was over and it was time to resume our work.
He had everything ready: deadbolt on the door,
windows bricked shut. He handed me a key,
stepped inside and closed the door, which I locked.

Nights I pressed my ear to the kitchen floor
to eavesdrop on suffering's heartbeat.
Sentimental songs on a staticky AM station.
And sometimes, yes, the Russian humming along.

"SCIENTISTS TO DETERMINE WHY JOHN WAYNE GACY BECAME SERIAL KILLER; BRAIN WILL BE REMOVED AFTER EXECUTION"

—The San Francisco Chronicle May 18, 1994

After the TV crews packed up,
the doctors in charge
got bored quick—*Try to find a needle*

in a haystack the size of Venus—
and plopped the tattered gray gob
back into its bucket. But grant checks

had been cashed: some token slicing
was required. An intern pulled
the short straw from the offered fistful

of short straws, proceeded down
the long stairs to the lab
equipped with microscopic scissors

and a magnifying glass. The procedure?
Tedium's epitome, but simple enough: snip
open a cell, peer inside. *Whiskey*

*in this one. Here's a Chevy pickup: late
sixties, looks like.* The unlucky intern
grows old, dies, is replaced, and the soft ham

of nerves still glistens on the marble,
barely half carved. There are epiphanies—
dendrite for *knife* found wedged

between *apple* and *hair,* then *crawlspace*
two years later near *thread*—but they don't connect,
won't add up, and one night

the current intern, flabby, pale, with an air
of formaldehyde, notes in his log *It could be anyone!*
and lays his locked head on the slab to sleep.

THE PLASTIC SURGEON'S WIFE

over the years was sculpted lovelier
and lovelier: lips pillowed, buttocks lifted
to a tight split peach. When her body

was flawless, pure leopard, he began
experiments. He tried time-release
injections—vanilla bean, lilac, rose—

and her skin exhaled a steady hum of faint,
sweet murk. He was encouraged, went
further: tuned her vagina until they came

together every time. Streamlined her intestines.
In collaboration with a Johns Hopkins team
he mapped out a plan for total hair transplant

which went off without a hitch. By now her beauty
was inexpressible: poets scrambled to invent
new words. New schools of sculpture sprang up.

And through all the rage and furor floated
the plastic surgeon's wife, a galaxy
of tangerine mist. Until one morning,

freshly bathed, ripe cherry perched in her mouth
like a finch, she made a final stroke
with her nail file and struck the ceiling of beauty.

She struggled against it like a salmon
at a dam, but her husband confirmed
she could be no lovelier, inside or out.

Over the following weeks, slowly at first,
he began to flick his famous scalpel
among the giggling breasts and legs

of his secretaries, while his wife lay frantic
on her custom-made Botticelli clamshell bed,
searching in vain for overlooked moles,

tiny laugh lines, a final wisp of hair
left unbleached, unwaxed, and unplucked
above the bruised purple fig of her lip.

THE WHITE ANGEL PHARMACY

The pharmacist, a red-faced burgher swollen
with schnitzel and beer, watches young Georg Trakl,
his new apprentice, slip a handful of vials

in his pocket. The stealing doesn't bother him
much. Cocaine comes cheap. The trouble
is the boy's demeanor: thin and twitchy, nervous

as a squirrel. Customers expect to see health
in his shop, not sunken eyes and pale hands
trembling with powder. And even worse,

the talking. The boy's mouth foams with nonsense:
golden boats on black lakes, a red wolf strangled
by an angel, and always dark eagles: *Circling,*

circling, he says. It can't go on, the burgher thinks,
and that afternoon he lets the boy go. The poet
walks the icy streets of Salzburg, ears stinging

with bells and verses, voices shouting down
voices, his head frantic as a wasp's nest.
A whore crooks her finger from a doorway

and he follows her upstairs, drops a coin
in the chipped blue bowl. She begins to unbutton
her blouse. *No, no, Angel,* he cries. *Just sit! Sit*

and listen. And his wild remedy whirls out at her
like a blizzard down from the mountains, mad
to cancel the unbearable world with white.

"KELLY, RINGLING BROS. OLDEST ELEPHANT, GOES ON RAMPAGE"

— *The New York Times* February 3, 1992

Her reasons for snapping seem clear: barbed tip
of the whipcord, squirming toddler cargo
glopping Sno-Cone on her back, cramped freight cars,
stale hay, the vet's incessant vitamin shots . . .
Or maybe it was boredom. Think of all the circles
she wore into the earth. Twenty-seven years of plod,
orbiting the Ringmaster's megaphoned jokes
while squads of ballerinas dug their heels
into her spine. Perhaps it wasn't pain
but repetition: the routine—balance beachball
on trunk-tip, wag ears—as sure and dull
as gravity. The question then is not why

but why today? Why that exact instant to rage
through the bleachers, tossing clowns like peanut husks,
sending dozens of kids to nightmare clinics?
What spark or fulcrum, what sudden volition
rose like a bubble through her four tamed tons
and burst in her meaty head?

After all, means of escape are always
at hand. Nothing remarkable
about shotgun triggers or train tickets,
the hard part is when to use them.
You yourself, right now, with a few
well-placed blows, could knock your world down
to the pile of boards it started as,
pick up a hammer and begin again from scratch:

move to Phoenix, raise cattle, change your name.
The brittle unbearable rests in your palm.
Will you close your fist or won't you, and why?
They shot her forty times before she died.

PAPERS

The ancient Russian refugee drifts off,
lolling his withered head against
the wheelchair's pillow. His tiny room
at the Ben Gurion Home for the Aged
is knee-deep with papers: towers of boxes,
mildewed folders, overflowing files.
Under the bathroom sink, a safe full
of passports. In '36 he crossed
into Finland with a forged one,
and two years later debarked in New York.
He began, as a hobby, collecting papers:
Russian transit vouchers, entry questionnaires
from Ellis Island, *cartes de séjour* . . .
He put ads in the *Times*, drove all over town
to buy the yellowing forms out of attics
and hatboxes. People shook their heads,
said *That paper saved my life*, then
Thank God I'll never need it again.
He diversified, bought Chinese exit visas,
a journalist's permit to enter Libya,
a day pass for West Berlin. Green cards,
a guarantee of passage on the last plane
to leave Luanda, a letter of transit
on lavender paper signed by Tito himself,
ID cards from Warsaw, Soweto, the Gaza . . .

Now the refugee jerks from sleep,
breathing in panicked gasps. His milky eyes
squint to focus on the boxes and drawers
stuffed with clearances and seals,
blurred purple stamps, the signatures

of so many ghosts. He sinks back,
relieved, pats absently for a cigar.
Let them come for me, he chuckles. *I can go*
anywhere. He shows the guard
from his dream his irrevocable visa
to sleep, lifts his empty suitcase, and steps across
the border, still half-
waiting for the bullet to explode in his throat.

ROSTROPOVICH AT CHECKPOINT CHARLIE, NOVEMBER 11, 1989

The maestro, in his Paris hotel, clicks
the television on. A girl with a purple mohawk
chops at the Wall with a hatchet, blasting

chunks of concrete and a cloud of gray dust
into the floodlit air. Beside her, a man in a tuxedo
jimmies his crowbar into a chink, hands his jacket

to someone in the crowd, and drives the bar down
with all his weight. Cracks spider up
through the motley graffiti. The mob roars.

Someone shouts *Mehr Licht!* and a hundred drunk
Berliners run for flashlights. The maestro checks
his watch, lifts the phone. Six hours later he steps from a taxi

onto Friedrichstrasse, just as dawn is staining
the sky. He buys coffee from a vendor and together
they survey the street's disaster: splintered

splits of champagne, heaps of broken stone tentacled
with steel, a woman's shoe, fast-food wrappers,
and the half-smashed Wall as a backdrop: dilapidated

curtain in an abandoned theatre. *Today all Berlin
will have a hangover,* says the vendor. *There are worse
afflictions,* Rostropovich replies. He has lived in exile

for sixteen years. *It's fine by me,* shrugs the vendor.
The hung-over buy coffee by the bucketful.
The maestro asks for a chair. The man finds a rusty one

and unfolds it with a creak. The maestro sits
in the shadow of the Wall, lifts his cello from its case, then
lunges, stabs the bow across the strings,

and instantly the street is possessed: Bach's Suite #5.
The chords circle low, wary as a flock of crows, then vault
into melody, retreat, begin again: threnody, aubade,

threnody, aubade, like a man who wakes up
on the morning he's longed for and finds he can think of
    nothing
but the night just ended and the night to come.

I I

What right do you have to live in a
house made of real materials, built by
genuine people?

—N. S. Khrushchev
to abstract painter B. Zhutovsky,
December 1, 1962

EXACTLY WHAT HAPPENED

O! answer me: let me not burst in ignorance!

—Hamlet to the Ghost

Because he must know exactly what happened, the cop
has a notebook the size of an atlas and scribbles continually
as you talk. You imagine yourself a brilliant young teacher,

the cop your dutiful pupil, and to ace the course he must capture
the man who mugged you, or, for a C, retrieve your soggy family
snapshots from a dumpster. And so today's lecture: *Exactly What
Happened.*

Outside the Paris Theatre on 58th, while Branagh's *Hamlet* unspooled
inside,
a man with a knife said two words, you forked over, he ran. The end.
Fled, the cop says. *We say "fled." And use "the suspect,"*

not "a man." Go on. Odd cop, you think, to stickle over diction so,
but to humor him you say sure, of course, the *suspect fled*
and his eyes were gray but greenish too, he was five-nine, heavyset,

Caucasian, blue jacket, greasy Green Bay Packers stocking cap.
O.K., the cops says, impatient. *You know what details are, pal?*
You ever heard of precision? Then let's have it. Start over.

You're sweaty now and aiming to please. You recall a skull
tattoo on the back of the suspect's left hand, his once-broken nose,
a voice surprisingly deep. Slight limp in left leg, an earring.

The cop's fully exasperated: *Buddy, this won't cut it.*
Make me feel like I was there! Put me inside your skin!
Force the whole kicking terror of that moment down my throat!

The officer has now manifested each of the psychosis symptoms
you recall from *DSM-IV.* You know you must be unbelievably clear
or risk his total break. So you paw through memory's vast trashcan,

grabbing rags and tin cans at random: icy drizzle, dull point
of the black-handled knife, two dusty white pigeons chuckling
in the gutter, the weirdly humiliating hard-on you got

just after the bastard ~~ran~~ fled, the tic you saw convulse
his cheek, the air a swampy funk of bus exhaust and piss,
Andrew Jackson smug on a twenty-dollar bill, the peanut

you choked on, its salt and soft meat, your wife crying
for Ophelia inside the theatre next to the empty seat
where you should be, the mugger's nonchalance saying *Give me*

in a gust of gin and hotdog breath, and the ridiculous
but ice-clear fear you felt handing the backpack over: *He'll see
what I've been reading and know* ~~what~~ *who I am.*

The cop grins: *Better! Better! You're getting the idea, pal!*
And this scant praise purrs down your spine like a Ferrari
because you're the student now: you'll yammer all day

about what never happened to make this man believe
it's exactly what did, and the cop, patient as a piano teacher,
says *Now try this for practice, kid: Describe me.*

MAY DAY, 1921, VITEBSK

Malevich and his students
hung huge white screens—each painted
with a single shape—
on street corners all over town.

A red circle in front of the butcher's.
A yellow triangle near the high school.
A blue circle on a garden fence.
A black square outside the mayor's house.

The students had asked to paint
all the streets red, but were refused
by the bewildered town council.
The screens constituted a compromise.

Poor middle-of-nowhere Vitebsk,
home to the new Soviet Academy of Art.
Odd sculptures towered in the square.
Wild chatter filled the tea rooms.

The morning the screens went up

a boy stumbled on a loose
cobblestone
and cut his hand

a newly-married girl
ruined three loaves of bread
by using too much yeast

and an old blind priest
heard the weeping of the boy
and the girl. *Who is playing*

that beautiful music, he called
out his window. *You are going to break
my heart!*

LAIKA

> *"Well, if he wishes it, I will, but I can no*
> *longer answer for anything," she thought, and*
> *rushed forward at full tilt. . . . She now*
> *scented nothing more, but only saw and heard*
> *without understanding anything.*

— Laska, Levin's dog, in *Anna Karenina*

Ignition shudders down her bones, the slow, thick hand
of thrust begins to press her head
into her neck, and the capsule goes black

with roar, her stomach hitching up at each abrupt
drop as the rocket's stages burn out, fall
back. Pressure forces vomit through her snout, her ears

are packed with clamor, and then the sound snaps
off like a bent branch cracking
at last. She rises from her harness and breathes.

The presses at Pravda clack all night. Khrushchev dances
giggling drunk in his nightshirt and Ike
stays home from church. Reporters jostle shoulder

to shoulder in Oppenheimer's office, scribbling notes,
children in Nebraska are drilled to dive
under desks if the sky flashes white, every wall

in the Pentagon is plastered with charts and maps
and Californians rush to backyards with binoculars
as all America scrambles to translate

Laika's simple message: a steady beep: her heartbeat.
To her alone, afloat in the no-world of the capsule, it means
only what it means: blood's thick course. She suckles

protein from a tube in her chest. She paddles
at the nothing. She does not imagine rabbits. If
she thinks, she thinks, *How lucky to be done*

with all that noise. Now the gauge on the air tank
wavers into red. The cold inside strains to join
the cold outside. Her mind drifts into snow.

CONSERVATORY POND, CENTRAL PARK, NEW YORK, NEW YORK

The model yachts contend in seas sheltered
from any wave while their captains fidget
on the concrete shore, fingers sticky

with ice cream and Cracker Jack, less intrigued
by the tiny jibs and rudders of their ships
than their grandfathers would like.

Beyond the armada, on the far shore,
a flock of birders flutters into view.
They snap together telescopes and tripods,

screw four-foot lenses into cameras,
and vanish in a thicket of magnification
just as their quarry, a red-tailed hawk, dives

from his nest high above Fifth Ave., snatches
a squirrel off the grass not ten feet away,
and banks into an oak to eat. Equipment

superfluous, the birders stare up rapt.
The crowd grows fast: yuppies on mountain bikes,
Haitian nannies pushing strollers, some drunks,

the young skippers, their rankled guardians.
Fifty heads tilt and swivel like radar
as the hawk drags its prey from branch to branch.

A woman in a filthy Mets sweatshirt
stops tossing popcorn to the chipmunks, screams
Drop it, fucker! Go back to the goddamn forest!

She hurls rocks, misses. But the hawk, flustered,
bobbles, and the torn gray rag falls
at her bandaged feet. Guts shiny with blood. Eyes

augered out. The crowd looks around. We see
how close we're standing, begin to inch apart.
In the pond, the abandoned boats collide, go down.

UNIVERSAL STUDIOS BACKLOT,
LOS ANGELES, CALIFORNIA

for David Conley

When his first Hollywood job—post production
on a cop drama—wrapped, everything vanished
overnight: gate pass, office, paycheck, even

the flick, which some unseen producer,
with a wave of his Partagas, sent straight
to Asian video. But we were in town

for just a week and pleaded to see the studio,
so Dave took us down to the lot, revved
his old golf cart to a dental-drill whine

and blew by the guard with a crisp salute.
Remember L.A. rule one, he said, checking
the rearview for trouble. *To seem is to be.*

Nowhere was this clearer than on the tour
we took that day, where a sharp left
in ancient Rome could land you in Brooklyn,

on a street of plywood brownstones hung
with lemon slabs of sun. Under a fake fire hydrant
I found a mound of sawdust and cigarette butts.

Later we passed the pond where Jaws still lurks
in his gloom of algae. At each passing tour bus
he breaches with an awkward hydraulic lurch,

wretched as Norma Desmond, chipped gray teeth
scary as a basketful of kittens, i.e., not very.
The tourists weren't even watching; they were

looking at us. A guy in a *Titanic* T-shirt
swiveled his camera our way, slowly, so as not
to spook us, cool as a big game hunter

taking a bead on a wildebeest. *We're young,*
wearing sunglasses, and driving a golf cart on the lot,
said David, waving. *We are movie stars.*

So I did my part for Hollywood: contorted
forward in my seat, smiled with all my teeth,
sank back into fame's exhausted green water.

STEVE'S COMMANDO PAINTBALL,
SAN ADRIANO, CALIFORNIA

NO RED AMMO spells a tin sign screwed
to an oak. I ask the owner why. *It stains,* he says.
He pockets my twenties, thrusts

a heavy black gun into my hands, barks down
the list of rules: no close-range fire,
goggles on at all times, etc. *Sissy stuff,*

he adds, apologetic. I load up my gumball
bullets, unbloody yellows and greens.
A burst of full-auto—like popcorn—echoes

from the practice range. I'm here to chaperone
six kids from the school where I teach.
They haven't done this before, but assured me

It's cool. I suggested mini golf. Fat chance.
When the plastic trumpet squawks to signal
the war's begun, they melt into the brush, lose

me instantly. So here I am, alone on a dazzled
spring morning high in the Santa Cruz mountains,
sweating under goggles, helmet, and face mask,

the redwoods full, I know, of salesmen and mechanics
who mean to point their guns at me and shoot. I buy it quick,
in the stomach, a bee sting under my sweater, and trudge

to the Dead Zone, fingering the wet white blot
and yelling as I've been taught: *Dead man! Dead man
coming through!* This keeps you from dying twice.

You can smoke once you're dead. And there are chairs.
The afterlife is bounded by orange traffic cones.
A teenage St. Peter with walkie-talkie checks your weapon

when you enter. *Safeties on in the Dead Zone!*
he scolds, if a corpse wanders in with his gun still hot.
I talk with a travel agent from San José.

Though allegiance means nothing to the dead,
I'm glad his armband matches mine. *Every human
has the instinct to hunt,* he says. *Better to get it out here*

than go psycho in McDonald's or the post office.
The trumpet blares for rapture, and we rise from our seats.
One of my kids turns up with his throat shot blue.

Having fun? I ask. He nods. Solemn. Says *Yes I am.*

JULY 4: AT LITTLE BIGHORN BATTLEFIELD, MONTANA

Our Cheyenne guide struggled with his microphone
on the Visitor Center patio, his talk—of troop
movements, ridges, retreats—ripped

by screeches of feedback. We got the gist:
we could see the rows of tombstones
from our seats, each with a small snapping flag.

The tour traces Custer's advance in reverse,
from the knoll where he died to the lookout point
where he spotted the Indian lodges, as if

we could reassemble the man as we walked, correct
each mistake, send him back up Rosebud Creek
ignorant and intact. *The last major Indian victory,*

shouted our guide. We could barely hear him
above the hot, howling wind. Two teenagers
in our group left the trail, lit sparklers, waved

the bright hissing wands like signals
toward the herd of motor homes parked below.
Our guide ran back, yanked them to the blacktop trail.

We heard only scraps of his speech—*rattlesnake,*
brush fire, relics—but his meaning was as clear
as the insolent pouts on the faces

of the kids. He was begging them to leave
his country and his people in peace,
and they were saying never, never, never.

AIDS HOSPICE, HOUSTON, TEXAS

The wraiths who live next door rise before dawn
to trudge, bent over canes, the gravel walks
of the hospice's small and weedy lawn,

single file, silent, a band of bathrobed monks.
No, not monks. Nothing holy. This is death
unmysterious: just tedious months,

time to become a student of your health,
chart daily bloodwork results, research herbs,
and come, perhaps, to wonder at the stealth

of the tiny murderer which surges
through your veins in merciless, lavish swarms.
It is, somehow, perfect: pure savage urge.

The youngest one (they are all young), still gorgeous
in his muscle-shirt, looks up, sees me through the glass.
He smiles, half-waves, stops, turns bashful. The sun

breaches the freeway overpass and blasts
its queasy heat into the yard. The men stagger
in the sudden brilliance. Smolder. Vanish.

YOCTOSECOND

A yoctosecond, equivalent to
.0000000000000000000000001 seconds,
is the smallest designated unit of time.

Smidgen of plankton snagged in history's baleen,
single brick in the Gotham of a second,
eyelash in the drain of an instant's kitchen sink.

What could happen in one of these? To snap
your fingers would take billions, the whorls
of your thumb and forefinger groaning over

each other yocto- by yocto- like a lead-laden
freight train chuffing up an Alp. Ditto shooting stars,
hummingbird hearts, a fastball's trip from mound

to mitt, a tornado rearranging Main Street,
the camera shutter's click. All things we think
firecracker-quick take eons and eons of these.

Yet it seems some obsessive chronographer had need
of the thing. What flashbulbed his retina,
what flickered across his synaptic firmament

that required time sliced this thin to clock it?
The knife-thrower's wrist-flick? A cobra or lightning
strike? A bullet dismantling a skull?

Or imagine the watchmaker on his deathbed: his last
whole second passes as he labors with his daintiest tools,
etching ever-finer lines between the numbers,

while Zeno's black arrow speeds home half by half.

THE MURDERED'S HOUSE

I did not know the murdered man,
but his red house across the street
is like an old friend.
When I glance up from the morning papers to think,
there it is outside my window, thinking too.

About much larger things,
I'm sure,
than the day's little troubles.

Last winter a cardinal starved to death
in its yard. I said to the red house,
From high above, you too
must look like a frozen cardinal
in a snowy front yard,
and the blue houses like jays,
and the brown ones wrens!

It can't make much difference
to the murdered's house
that this tenant left to the sound of sirens
instead of farewells and nostalgic songs,
that there was no room for books
or chairs in his moving van.
It can't make much difference either
that he left before his lease was up.

The new roomer will move in soon
with his rags and caged canary,
the greasy sack of tools he needs
to ply his crucial trade.

CHICKEN TRUCK

Straight out of *Grapes of Wrath*, wrought from God
knows how many dead Fords, the chicken truck
sputters in the slow lane toward Chicago,
its teetering stacks of wire crates packed

with proto-cutlets, Kentucky-Fried-to-be.
Clouds of down and dander billow behind
like a slumber party gone haywire.
As I pass doing eighty it's impossible

to discern *birds:* the swaying wall of white
is continuous as milk, unbroken
by any singular wing or beak. The hungry city
sharpens its long, unanimous knife.

A prairie gust shoves the chicken truck
smack into my lane. I veer, re-veer,
and my own sullen cargo opens its black eyes
like two empty cupboards, then closes them again.

KHRUSHCHEV'S SHOE

Under a jumble of oxfords and pumps,
half-stuffed in a boot someone once dyed blue,
eerie as a chunk of uranium

in a briefcase: Premier Khrushchev's right shoe.
The Cyrillic label removed all doubt:
this was the shoe he smacked on the UN

lectern in 1960, drowning out
the bewildered Mexican delegate
and driving America underground

with sacks of canned peaches and first aid kits.
With a temper like that, went the thinking,
what's to stop him from nuking St. Louis?

How his shoe wound up in a Goodwill bin
of golf spikes, galoshes, and mismatched clogs
I did not know or care. I gave two bits

to the clerk and was handed back a bag
of the twentieth century, size 12.
In a flash I foresaw problems with Prague.

I stormed back home, put some soup on the stove,
ordered the army into Budapest.
I blocked publication of *Dr. Zhivago,*

but allowed *Ivan Dinisovich* past.
I shook my fist at a pinup of Nixon,
woke my neighbor at three a.m. to request

an apology for the U-2 missions.
I gloated over Sputnik. Soon I'd pushed
everyone into line: even the mailman

said "Mr. Premier." But what next? What fresh
world remained to be sculpted to my will?
I would go to Moscow, reclaim my office,

lead Russia to glory again! The streets were filled
with crowds—to welcome me! But then I saw.
Hundreds of them, from every nation,

each with one shoe, declaring martial law,
their cries white-hot in the January air
that even then showed no sign of a thaw.

50¢

for Brent Goodman

Not enough to be a burden (hardly cause
to open that offshore account), but sufficient
to feel you're just this side of zilch,

one degree above zero on poverty's thermometer,
and that you have *options:* can of cola,
admission to the petting zoo, two phone calls.

Not a weight but a fulcrum: a speck but a speck
upon which everything might turn. Tycoon spots
half-dollar under gum wrapper in gutter,

stoops to pinch it in his chalk stalk fingers,
thus nudges his portfolio past billionaire.
Buys a Jaguar to celebrate and, martini-dizzy,

takes a swan drive off a cliff. Across town,
the Hungarian viola tutor who dropped the coin
comes up four bits short on the rent, has to hock

his fiddle, takes up semiconductor design,
makes a mint. Tonight at O'Cayz Corral,
the handmade signs for string cheese, ear plugs,

aspirin, and happy hour drafts all say *50¢.*
If you were starving, a pickled egg could save you.
Here, have one. My buck will buy two.

STORY

The cops locked the windows when they left,
so when I arrived at the junkie's apartment
to scour her story from the walls
and countertops, the air

was hot and thick as stew. Dog
stew. I would be paid twenty dollars
by my boss the slumlord
for spending my Saturday erasing the maps

of mold she left in the refrigerator,
the glyphs of her kid's broken toys
strewn across the bedroom floor,
and as a bonus, a non-taxable tip,

I'd get to read the place before I bleached it,
see what everyone in that small town
would love to have seen: the front-page drug den
where the daughter of the mayor of a neighboring town

bound her two-year-old with extension cord
and smacked herself dead.
I found a full can of beer in the oven
and a photograph of a radio

taped inside the medicine chest.
A nurse's uniform on a wire hanger
in the otherwise empty closet.
There was no mention of these clues

in the newspaper, and though I'm no cop
and not much of a reporter, I thought these things
might matter, so I memorized them, I made them
a story, before I scrubbed the place clean.

I I I

Your feates and trickes then must be nimbly,
cleanly, and swiftly done, and conveyed so as
the eyes of the beholders may not discerne or
perceave the tricke, for if you be a bungler,
you both shame your selfe, and make the Art
you goe about to be perceaved and knowne,
and so bring it into discredit.

—Samuel Rid, in *The Art of Jugling, or
Legerdemaine,* 1612

THE FUTURE

Pick a card, bellowed the parking lot attendant,
offering a fanned-out deck across the shelf
of his kiosk's Dutch door. Block-lettered
over the heart-spot of his red company jumpsuit
was the lot owner's slogan: *TRUST THIS MAN.*
I was late for work. But if this aspiring prestidigitator
needed a guinea pig upon which to practice his craft,
O.K., I could do that. I drew—jack of hearts—
and moved to slip it back into the deck, but the old man
snatched it from my fingers and slapped it down face up.
I will now tell your future, he thundered,
pressing the card beneath his meaty palm
and studying the bridge of my nose with a frown,
as if it were under suspicion. *This very day,*
he cried, *you will die a horrible death!*

Each morning that summer on my way to work
I'd pause to pick the day's fate from his deck.
Some days he'd smile at my card, assure me
I'd be worth billions by sunset, more often
that I'd better call my mother one last time.
On the last night of August I stopped
at his twilit shack, noted aloud
that I had once again eluded death,
and put it to him straight: Why did he persist
in his predictions? Clearly none came true.
He let out his carny-barker belly laugh.
Young friend, I don't tell fortunes to be right,
that would be nuts! No one can know what comes next!

The day was nearly done. Next came night.
We shared a smoke in the dying air
which already smelled of tomorrow, where yet again—
we know it for certain—
the anything that always happens will.

CONJURER'S HONOR

I.

My pal the struggling sculptor, poor as dirt,
at last got a break: a State of Missouri commission
for busts of three famous sons: Truman, T. S. Eliot,

and Disney. A few months later I visited his studio,
a tiny walk-up crammed with his work—bronze
skulls, ribcages, femurs, clavicles, eerily exact—

and his grisly models: box upon box of human bones.
I never asked where they came from. He never said.
Each burnished skeleton, once assembled, was named

for a massacre: *My Khe, Mountain Meadows, Glencoe,
Sand Creek* . . . In fifteen years he'd sold only one: *Kishinev,*
to B'nai B'rith's New York headquarters. *I pray*

you run out of subject matter soon, the Director had said,
but his check ran out first. So my friend took
the Missouri commission for wax and plaster money.

Over beers he said president and poet were done,
crated and shipped to St. Louis. But the Show-Me State
would not release funds until Disney was delivered, and this

was a problem. The forehead was wrong. *See for yourself,*
he said, drawing the cloth from Walt's stone head.
I compared it with the photo. It looked fine to me.

Besides, I said, it's only for some dusty niche in Missouri,
only for money. *Not the point,* said my pal. *The man's forehead
is wrong.* But what about your real work? I said. What Minerva

sprang from this brow that it should warrant such attention?
The lisping duck? The pie-eyed mouse? My friend cut me off.
It's magician to magician, see? It's conjurer's honor.

II.

> *Disney's preoccupation with his mortality led
> him to explore the science of cryogenics.
> He often mused about the notion of having
> himself frozen.*
>
>   Marc Eliot, in *Walt Disney: Hollywood's Dark Prince*

The janitor, an out-of-work comedian,
props his mop among the garlands

of hoses screwed to the capsule,
takes a stub of chalk from his coverall, scrawls

DisneyTank™ on the dull gray hull.
He could get fired, sure, but the joke

is worth the risk, even depends upon it—
the things we'd never dare do

comedians do for us. Magicians
have it even harder: they do

what we've never imagined.
Think of Disney, asleep in liquid air,

blood laced with glycerin, brain gone
stone. It isn't true: he was cremated.

But his triumph is the rumor, our wish
to believe he's in there, locked

tighter than Houdini, plotting
the ultimate illusion. The janitor

has complained of spooky noises: clanks
and pings from the tank. His boss says

Don't be an idiot. Steel expands
or contracts if there's a temperature shift.

But knowing doesn't matter. At the slightest squeak
the comic flicks his eyes to the rusting hatch

and waits for the impossible,
inevitable turn.

III.

*We are not saying that you can't have a great
time at Walt Disney World. We are saying that
you need a plan.*

—Bob Sehlinger, in *The Unofficial Guide to
Disney World*

Some misguided sparrows cobbled together a nest
in the prestressed concrete branches
of the Swiss Family Robinson's tree.
The execs upstairs thought it harmless,

maybe even good for an AP human-interest photo,
and voted to let the birds stay. Next
came the tentworms. Tiny white fingers
flexing up the handrails of the staircase,

falling from their gauzy kingdoms into strollers,
down souvenir T-shirts. This was bad for biz.
Next morning the air was tinted with kerosene,
and the worms had vanished. But later the same week,

all at once, came eighteen squirrels, clear evidence
of termite activity, and a greenish woodpecker
which the Orlando Audubon Society identified
as endangered. The boys upstairs called their wives

and ordered takeout. Terrified, they argued
and blamed, until one senior assistant
to a junior vice-president stopped cold and said
Termites? The damn thing's made of stone!

Outside, in the October Florida moonlight,
the tree's vinyl leaves were turning yellow.
One by one they loosed from the boughs
to litter the asphalt below, like the countless

crumpled playbills the dead drop as they rise.

NIXON DEAD

On Nixon's first night in the ground, worm
constituents inching up to shake his hand,
workers are wrenching together the Ferris wheel

for San Francisco's annual carnival.
I walk among them in the fog
of yellow headlights, apple brandy, curses

spat from beneath their greasy caps.
The City Hall flag hangs limp at half-mast, as if
exhausted with grief. In '72

we gave him our hearts like a bucket
of baseballs. Tonight, in this air choked
with diesel, loud with the clang

of hammers on iron, I think of his casket descending
on the wide canvas straps: his final trick
a disappearing act, like everyone's.

The Ferris wheel teeters upward, its galaxy
of red and yellow bulbs flashing
against the stars. An Arkansas carny

sets up his Shoot-the-Duck stand. Kewpie dolls
hang by their hair on rusty hooks. He asks
if I wanna free ride. I answer *Who wouldn't?*

The basket sways and creaks as I rise
and fall: going nowhere, but thrilled to be released
and returned, released and returned, lucky

as Lazarus. The carny pulls a lever, stops me
at the top. I hear screaming far below.
The sleight-of-hand man, sawing his mistress in two.

ZOO FIGHT

We pledge our "really sorries"
in the bamboo portico

not because we are but because
the spat's stalled: rebuttals spent,

agon intact as ever.
In the half-lit Primate Hut

kids scratch their armpits and scream
at chimps, who, of course, scream back.

Tile walls multiply the din.
You tick your head side to side

like Beethoven's metronome,
keeping rage's steady time.

In a dirty case lit red,
a black fist of fur picks gnats

from his mate's back. *Tamarins,*
I say. You say *Marmosets.*

The dark heat creeps up our throats.
But the plaque says a third thing,

some beast we've never heard of.
They gawk with idle malice,

toss their dung at us, the glass.
Your fingers weave into mine.

The monsters cling together
in their artificial night.

HOUDINI

This is God's work: before a jeering crowd,
cigars fuming beneath hat brims,
to be mummified in chains, crated, and shot
from a cannon into the river. *Dead,*
says the faithless one, the rationalist
near the railing, *res ipsa loquitur.*
The bubbles come up. The world worlds and all is well.
A stranger taps his shoulder for a light. He turns
and it is I, hair damp beneath my hat,
cigar bone dry in my trembling hand.

There is no magic here, no trick, no world
beneath the one you see. I never crept
unseen into the wings. It was me in that casket
launched from the bridge, no effigy.
To escape I loosed nails with my teeth
while freezing water choked
down my throat. Look at these fingers,
cut and callused stalks. Look at these arms,
the exhausted rubber muscle. This
is God's work: to trick you
into magic not through illusion or divinity,
but by beating my scant and bleeding hands
against the darkness—and worse and more
important: never to be fooled myself.

UPON SEEING AN MRI IMAGE
OF MY BRAIN

for Wil Irwin

First comes a panicky craving for similes—
ghost of dusty birdcage, river delta
pictured by spy satellite, oriental fan made of ham—

next the seeping realization that each of these
(plus the need itself to dream them up) sparked to life
from somewhere in there, like matches struck in a stadium.

How could this lopsided gob of meat emit something
subtle as *schadenfreude*, exact as a hankering
for eggplant? You step from under an awning,

snug in your raincoat, into an April thunderstorm.
A tremor of pleasure (part womb-wish, part atavistic
need-for-shelter) flashes down your bones, and

bang! you think of Rilke's panther, the image
that enters his eye, shivers through his taut limbs
and vanishes into the heart. (Meanwhile,

sotto voce, the olfactory newswire is reporting
lilac and dogshit.) How many neural musicians
have parts in *that* millisecond symphony, and where

in this grayscale blur is their orchestra pit? This stunted
butterfly in the center? That jaundiced fig?
One of these inlets or knuckles? I'm not playing dumb;

I know the lingo. This notch a sulcus, these hills gyri,
these respective doodads the thalamus, pons, medulla oblongata.
We know some things about them. Mostly we don't.

I have flown over the ocean at night, when the moon
limned the vast blank surface with silver,
and believed the obsidian sheen beneath me, expressing

nothing, had nothing to express. Believe this or that,
as you wish. Tonight, like every night, the sea
is seized just underneath with pressure and menace.

AMTRAK CLUB CAR, 3:30 A.M., NEAR PITTSBURGH, PENNSYLVANIA

It's about a kid who hates his father.
It's a true story. The man in the corner
of the club car who's been scribbling all night,
sucking pencils and three-dollar cans of beer,

is now drunk enough to tell us the truth.
The five of us look up from books, restless
sleep, our various forms of solitaire,
shift in our seats, settle in to listen.

We're tired of our own stories—the termites
and cramps of them, the way they never change—
but still we keep them, like inmates read letters
they've known by heart for years. A mining town

presents its empty streets for our approval.
The man looks out the window, back
to his yellow pad dark with lead, then shouts—
his voice loud, slurred—*It's the first important thing*

I've ever written. Again we all look up.
The pretty blind woman in the sunflowered dress
even nods slightly, as if to urge him on,
but she's misread his voice. She's nodding at me.

HENRY MILLER MEMORIAL LIBRARY, BIG SUR, CALIFORNIA

Just a tumbledown two-room shack at the end
of a dirt driveway which wanders in from Route 1.
In the yard iron sculptures rust under redwoods
twenty times their height. Brown lizards squirt
across the rotting porch, blink in sunlight,
vanish. A fat teenage visitor, studying the books
for sale—none may be borrowed, I notice—
exclaims to her bored, pimply boyfriend,
Everyone knows Anaïs wrote most of this!

It is foolish to make things up in the mountains.
What wouldn't look puny against this landscape?
Trees thick as houses, meadows stunned
with wildflowers sweeping in vast green strokes
to the dizzying edges of cliffs, ocean punishing
the boulders below with its incessant chant
of weight and salt. . . .
But Miller had the nerve to try, this man
who thought his cock the axis of all eros.

My companion and I hike down the road
into deserted Partington Canyon. She is heavy
with her period, which is when I love her most.
On a flat rock under white sun we hold
a memorial of our own, a kind of conversation
about the earth that leaves us dazed and glowing
with blood. *Isn't the west a sacred place,*
she says. A statement, not a question,
which is lucky for me: I don't know the answer.

SPACE MEMORABILIA AUCTION, SUPERIOR STAMP AND COIN, BEVERLY HILLS, CALIFORNIA

for Jim Richardson

When I bid my wad—forty bucks—on a helmet
with smoked-glass faceplate
and Soviet hammer and sickle stenciled

over the ears in—what else?—red,
I assumed I'd be outdone. But no one lifted
an eyebrow or wiggled a finger—not

the medal-spangled Air Force colonel, not the bored
old actress in pink chiffon, not her poodle,
also pink. Imagine my triumph when the gavel fell,

but still, I wondered, what gives?
A single foil pouch of freeze-dried ice cream product
had gone for three grand just minutes ago.

I asked the guy next to me what was up,
and he explained through his cucumber sandwich
my helmet was training-camp stuff,

prototypical—in short, it had never left
the earth. I had stumbled on the odd economy
of space memorabilia: value rests not

in what, but how far. Thus no one bid a dime
for the set of Cape Canaveral silverware,
but a used washcloth from Mir nearly caused a riot.

Hilarious, I thought. Grown men and women
scribbling zero after zero on their chits
for golfballs, tubes of toothpaste, socks.

I wandered over to the display table
and tried on a glove from the Soyuz mission.
Used in three space walks, the catalog said.

Inside its eighteen heat-retaining layers
my hand felt suddenly absent, as if I'd thrust it
into another world. A quiet one. One above

all hungers, above the contorted atmosphere,
from which the earth would seem mercifully simple.
Yes, I thought, I'd buy this if I could.

WEST LOOP FREEWAY ON-RAMP, HOUSTON, TEXAS

Beside buckets of smog-jaundiced roses glowing
in the haze, forearm so carpet-bombed with track marks
it looked as if birds had pecked it to death,

he teetered on the curb with a Magic-markered sign:
Too Dollars. Like IV's of wealth, that purest dope,
the rush-hour on-ramps for the tony Galleria

were thick with Mercedes and Porsches queued to drip
into the freeway's fuming vein. As each crept by
he grinned, shook the blooms so their heads bobbed yes,

and each tinted window, sealed against the heat,
returned to him a still-life: junkie with bouquet.
My AC was shot. I had both windows open.

I didn't have too dollars to spare, but paid up anyway.
He thanked me a million, said he'd seen
my out-of-state plates: *My first sweetheart was from there.*

Touched, I said *Oh yeah?* The Jag behind me honked,
but it could wait for this. *Yeah,* he slurred back, *and man,
she was the ugliest damn bitch I ever fucked.*

I nodded like I knew what he meant. I may have
winked. I put it in gear, felt the clutch catch, angled
for a chance to take my place in traffic.

RESORT

Nothing could stay itself in that weather.
A bottle of gin turned to a hammer
and broke up the Dayton talks. Croquet drew blood.
We paddled halfway across the lake, floated back.
The radio said sirens might mean a test,
tornado, or war: it was up to us.

Drunk under the chalk tablet of the moon,
stumbling down the train tracks along the shore,
we found a corral of caution horses:
hundreds of roadblocks stacked behind barbed wire,
blinking their quick orange eyes at the dark.
If they're all here, nothing's dangerous.

I was by the lake reading a stack of newspapers
from obsolete countries when thunder punched the air,
shook the dock's rotten pylons beneath me.
I looked up for storm clouds and spotted
two bombers from the base up north, rumbling
up the bandage-white sky, tumid with rain.

THE YOUNG PHILOSOPHER

Walks through the bull's pasture
reading a book:
How to End Our Country's Suffering.

Half the chapters are short biographies
of famous magicians.
The others have titles like
"We Must Seize the Estate of Count S———."

The sun is the color
of cooked chicken. Or cooked egg.
He can't decide which.

The bull is famous in the village
for having killed eight men
in a single afternoon. It is as big
and black as a trawler in a storm.

The young philosopher
figures a syllogism on his fingers, nods
with decision. Lowers his head

and charges.

FRUIT FLY

Greg Knutson, R.I.P.

Harmless or not, I'd had it. Swarms rising
like smoke and ash from the bowl of bananas,
black galaxies swirling in the trash,
orgies in the juice, corpses in the jam.

I meant to kink their genes beyond repair,
to wreck their reproduction utterly,
and asked the K-Mart Garden Center clerk
for his most vicious insect killer.

He delivered instead a fruit fly education.
In six weeks of life each female makes eggs
by the thousands—does really nothing but.
Any poison I sprayed, bombed, or dusted

might take out millions, but I'd kill my cat
before the last fly tumbled with a tiny clunk.
There are . . . so *many* of them, said the kid,
vainly fluttering his hands through the air.

Walking back to my truck across the vast parking lot,
I thought of my mathematician pal. I'll bet
he would have loved these bugs, the genius
of their exponential reproduction, how they beat

mortality's rotten odds to a pulp. *For his sake,*
I thought, *I'll let them live.* But they lived
and died no matter what I did or didn't, flew
their short course and that winter vanished.

THE MISTAKES I MADE AND THE
THINGS I DID RIGHT

Remembering all the airports,
all the fights we drummed up
driving to the airports

since anger was needed to lift the pale lever,
set the thin string between us
spinning out . . .

One of us always turning
into smoke
against the hot white sky, and then,

once out of sight, just above the clouds,
changing again,
into a flock of swans.

Simple mistake:
we got the Buddha backwards, expected all
and slowly gathered nothing,

drank deep and deeper
into sky, until the sky turned
to air in our bitter mouths.

I want to hear the whole story now.
That last week's green tornado sky,
the white sky you climbed away through . . .

The mistakes I made. And the things I did right.

LAST REQUEST

A pine box for me. I mean it.

—My father

For the record, friends and family,
I'd like a pyramid when I go.

A small one is fine: build it
out of cardboard in the backyard.

For mortar use duct tape
or school glue: nothing strong enough

to make it sturdy. I want it
to fall down a lot. Lay me in there naked

on the shadowed grass and,
whatever the weather,

wait outside all night.
No beer, no burgers or dancing,

no horseshoes. You may smoke. Talk quietly
if you must talk. Be very sad.

The wind will push the pyramid over often.
Grumble as you set it back up.

Let it be a hard night. Be bored
and edgy. Snap at each other. Yawn.

Feel free to step inside my rickety tomb
to see me, say good-bye, but please: one at a time.

Just before dawn toss me and my pyramid
in the back of a pickup, drive us

to the dump, and dump us
on the tallest garbage mountain

you can find. It will be repulsive: flies
on my lips, old spaghetti sauce smeared

in my hair. Let it smell terrible.
Then go home. Quickly, before the cops show up

with their plastic bags and notebooks.
And on your way home, please

accept from me the only gift
I'll have to give: relief

you're not me. That even if this world
is a stagnant ditch between nothing

and nothing, you may at least
sip from it a little longer. Be glad,

and because I loved you,
forget me as fast as you can.

WHAT TO DO

Like a man at a bar before the rows
of brilliant bottles decides he wants not
to drink but simply to stand in the glow
of potential, I want to be content
with indecision, I wish to choose it.
The world demands I pick this or that, claims
it *matters,* that my choices determine
the GNP and weather, either save
the prisoner from the rack or stretch his guts
another notch. We forget every choice
annuls whole worlds we might have loved,
changes this one as little as one voice
in counterpoint to the mob's crude chant. Ignore
those starry torches. They go where they go.

ACKNOWLEDGMENTS

My thanks to the editors of the magazines in which some of these poems appeared, often in slightly different form:

5 AM: West Loop Freeway On-Ramp, Houston, Texas
Artful Dodge: Houdini; "Kelly, Ringling Bros. Oldest Elephant, Goes on Rampage"
Green Mountains Review: "Astronomers Detect Water in Distant Galaxy, Suggest Life May Be Present throughout Universe"; Story; The White Angel Pharmacy
Hurakan: Nixon Dead; The Murdered's House
Madison Review: Last Request
Nightsun: Khrushchev's Shoe
Northwest Review: Zoo Fight
Paris Review: Rostropovich at Checkpoint Charlie, November 11, 1989; "Scientists to Determine Why John Wayne Gacy Became Serial Killer; Brain Will Be Removed after Execution"
Phoebe: The Plastic Surgeon's Wife
Ploughshares: "Former Kenyan Parliament Member Arrested for 'Imagining the Death' of President Daniel arap Moi"
Press: Space Memorabilia Auction, Superior Stamp and Coin, Beverly Hills, California
Soundings East: Conjurer's Honor
Southwest Review: Snow
Sow's Ear Review: July 4: At Little Bighorn Battlefield, Montana
The Journal: Exactly What Happened
The Progressive: The Foreign Correspondent
Willow Springs: May Day, 1921, Vitebsk
Witness: Conservatory Pond, Central Park, New York, New York; Steve's Commando Paintball, San Adriano, California

Some of these poems were included in a chapbook, *This Just In,* published by Beyond Baroque Books (Los Angeles, 1998).

The poem "Lt. Shrapnel" appeared as a limited-edition chapbook published by Artichoke Yink Press (New York, 1999).

Many thanks to the Wisconsin Institute for Creative Writing for a year of support and fellowship.

Thanks also to Aaron Anstett, Francine Conley, Stephen Dobyns, Matt Freidson, Brent Goodman, Richard Howard, Wil Irwin, Jeff McDaniel, Cynthia MacDonald, Sarah Messer, Ellen Terrell, Steve Timm, James Wagner, Ron Wallace, and Adam Zagajewski for their editorial assistance. Particular thanks to Mary Karr, teacher and friend — *in illo tempore et hoc tempore.*